Plant Atlas

Table of Contents

Different kinds of plants grow in very different kinds of places. For example, African violets grow in cool, moist mountain forests. You would never see one in a desert. The barrel cactus does grow in deserts. It is never found in forests.

African violet

The shady, cool, moist soils of mountain forests are just right for the African violet. The barrel cactus is **adapted** to survive in the sunny, hot, dry climate of the desert. If you planted a barrel cactus in a mountain forest, it wouldn't live very long.

Do you grow any plants in your home? What do your plants need to stay alive?

barrel cactus

3

Although plants live in many different places, they all need the same basic things. They need water, soil, air, and light to live and grow. Of course, they do not all need the same kinds of soil or the same amounts of water, air, and light. For example, a cactus needs a lot of light, but not much water. Some other kinds of plants can grow without much light, but need a lot of water.

The conditions needed for plant growth are determined by climate. Regions of the world have different climates. These climates support plants and animals that are adapted to survive there. The regions of Earth that have their own kind of climate, soil, plants, and animals are called **biomes** (BYE-ohmz).

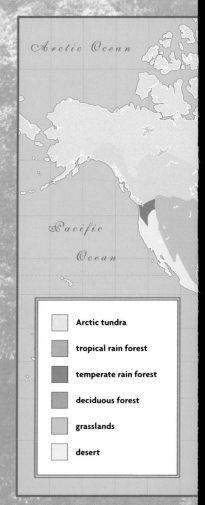

Arctic Ocean

Pacific
Ocean

- Arctic tundra
- tropical rain forest
- temperate rain forest
- deciduous forest
- grasslands
- desert

BIOMES OF THE WORLD

Scientists recognize many biomes. Those discussed in this book are highlighted in color. Biomes in the gray areas are not mentioned here.

Arctic tundra

Plants can be found everywhere in the world where there is enough water and sunlight to keep them alive. In the **Arctic** region near the North Pole is an open, flat, cold biome called the tundra. Plants grow even in this very cold place. The tundra winters are cold and long. The summers are cool and short.

Most tundra plants are small. They grow close to the ground in order to keep their branches and leaves out of the freezing cold wind. The wind is so cold, it could kill the plants. Rocks provide shelter from the wind, so some Arctic plants grow between the cracks of rocks.

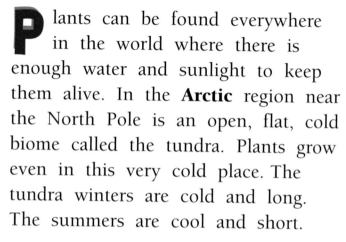

Despite the cold, some flowering tundra plants do bloom during the short summer.

Snow covers willows on the tundra in Manitoba, Canada.

Other plants grow right on the rocks. These are called **lichens**. Some Arctic lichens are thought to be 4,000 years old. Lichens aid in soil formation. They help make it possible for other Arctic plants to grow.

Rust-colored lichens grow over the entire surface of a limestone rock in the Arctic National Wildlife Refuge, Alaska.

It's a FACT!

- The average temperature in winter at the United States Arctic National Wildlife Refuge near Fairbanks, Alaska, is -10° Fahrenheit (-23° Celsius).

- The average temperature in summer is 62° Fahrenheit (17° Celsius).

tropical rain forest

Tropical rain forests grow near the equator, an imaginary line that runs around the middle of Earth. They are found in Africa and Asia. The largest rain forest in the world is found in South America. It rains very often in this hot, humid biome.

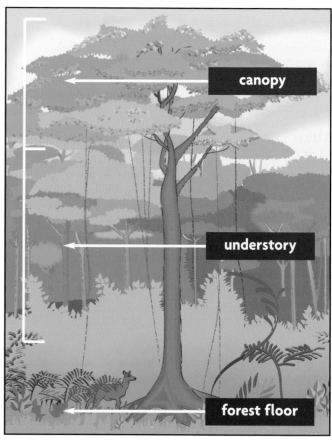

canopy

understory

forest floor

This is the understory of a tropical rain forest in Ecuador.

Rain forest trees spread their branches in the canopy to capture as much light as possible.

At the top of the rain forest is the **canopy,** where there is plenty of sunlight. Below the canopy are the understory and the forest floor, where it is shady.

These different parts of the rain forest provide perfect growing conditions for many different kinds of plants. And the plants provide homes for many different kinds of animals.

NATURE PROTECTORS

Name: The Nature Conservancy

Mission: The Nature Conservancy is the largest private international conservation group. Its goal is to preserve plants, animals, and the diversity of life on Earth.

Founded: 1951

Saving the Rain Forests: Through a program called Adopt An Acre, the Nature Conservancy raises money to purchase rain forest land. People who adopt an acre or more receive an honorary land deed. Although they don't actually own the land, they are directly involved in protecting it.

Have you ever eaten a fruit called a fig? Figs grow on trees that are found in the rain forest. Like all plants, fig trees need sunlight to grow. When fig trees are young and small, they grow slowly because there isn't much sunlight in the shade of the larger trees around them. But when a taller tree falls over, it leaves an opening, or gap, for sunlight to stream through.

Then the young fig trees grow quickly upward toward the Sun. The fig tree that grows fastest will win the race. It will get all the sunlight in the gap for itself, and the other fig trees will die.

Sunlight peeks through a gap in the rain forest canopy in a national park in Costa Rica.

fig leaves

Once the winning fig tree has grown as tall as it can, it begins to spread out and become part of the canopy. It forms new branches with many leaves. These large leaves let the tree take in a lot of sunlight so it can grow even bigger.

All of those branches and big leaves are heavy, so the fig tree also spreads out down below. Its trunk gets thicker so that it can hold up the heavy leaves and branches. The tree forms special roots above the soil. These are called **buttress roots**. They help hold up the giant tree.

These are the buttress roots of a fig tree in a tropical rain forest.

Some of the plants on the forest floor don't grow tall. They stay down near the ground for their entire lives. These plants require less light than others. They are specially adapted for life under the trees. One such plant is the fan palm.

Fan palms have large, thin leaves that spread out as far as possible to capture light. They are called fan palms because their leaves are pleated like a fan you might make out of paper.

The pleats in the leaves of the fan palm make the large leaves strong so that they don't rip easily. The pleats also allow water to run down the grooves and off the leaves. At the end of each groove is a pointed tip. This is called a **drip tip**. It guides the rainwater away from the plant. Although plants need water, too much water can be just as bad as not enough!

It's a
FACT!

There are well over 3,500 known species of palm trees. Most of them grow deep in the rain forest.

fan palm leaves

Some plants in the rain forest don't begin their life on the forest floor. They grow high up in the canopy without soil. These are called **air plants**. Air plants grow when seeds carried by the wind land on tree branches. As these seeds sprout, their roots wrap around the tree branches.

These beautiful orchid flowers are air plants.

PLANT PROFILE

Name: tank bromeliad

Biome: The tank bromeliad grows as an air plant on the branches of tropical rain forest trees.

Interesting Facts: The tank bromeliad catches and holds water between the bases of its leaves, forming a pool that insects, spiders, and even frogs call home. The plant doesn't have to worry about drying out from the wind between rain showers because it can use the water in the pool.

The bromeliad holds water in its own tank.

4 The Temperate Rain Forest

temperate rain forest

Not all rain forests are found where the weather is tropical and warm. There are a few places in the world where heavy rain falls every day, but where the temperature is cool and mild. These biomes are called **temperate** rain forests. They are found along the northwestern coast of North America, the southwestern coast of South America, and in parts of Australia. The temperate rain forests are home to many kinds of plants.

This is a temperate rain forest: Olympic National Park, Washington.

CHAPTER 4

Just as in the tropical rain forest, the largest plants in the temperate rain forest are tall trees. But the trees that grow in temperate rain forests are even bigger than those in the tropical rain forest. They are not in danger of drying out because it rains almost every day and the air temperature is always cool. For these reasons, they can live and grow for a very long time. The old trees in the temperate rain forest are some of the tallest in the world.

PLANT PROFILE

Name: giant sequoia

Biome: The temperate mountain rain forests of California

Interesting Facts: Giant sequoia trees are closely related to redwood trees, but are even bigger and older. The oldest is 3,200 years old. The largest sequoia ever measured was 311 feet tall, 41 feet around, and weighed almost 3 million pounds! That's the same as 10 blue whales, 13 space shuttles, or 200 elephants.

A man and a woman on a horse, photographed around 1900, can fit in the undercut of a giant sequoia.

the small leaves of
a redwood tree

Many large redwood trees were once cut for wood,
but are now protected by law.

deciduous forest

In some parts of Australia, Asia, Europe, and North America there is not enough rain to create a temperate rain forest. Instead, the forests in these places are home to many **deciduous** (deh-SID-yoo-uss) **trees**. Deciduous trees are trees that drop their leaves in the autumn of every year. They are the opposite of **evergreen** trees, which do not lose their leaves at all.

↑ summer in a deciduous forest

← winter in a deciduous forest

The deciduous forest is always changing. The most beautiful season is autumn, when the leaves of the trees change colors before they fall off. During the cold weather, the tree "shuts down" to survive the winter. Now the tree does not have to feed the leaves during the cold weather.

autumn in a deciduous forest

PLANTS AND ANIMALS: FOREST PARTNERS

Some interesting relationships between plants and animals can be seen in the deciduous forest. For example:

- Many forest wildflowers produce shiny black seeds with a small white bump on the outside. Ants love to eat the white parts of the seeds. They drag the seeds underground to their nests. The ants get a tasty treat, and they leave the seeds in the soil, where more wildflowers will grow.

- Other forest plants, like the oak tree, produce hundreds of seeds each year. We call the seeds of oak trees acorns, and animals like squirrels love to eat them. But the squirrels cannot eat all the acorns. They bury the extras in the soil. Squirrels often forget where they buried the acorns. These forgotten seeds will stay in the soil and grow into new oak trees.

To understand how deciduous trees are adapted to their changing biome, take a look at the sugar maple. In summer, it is covered in big green leaves that capture lots of sunlight. The leaves use the sunlight to make food for the tree. But the leaves make more food than the tree needs, so it stores the extra food as a liquid in its trunk. The liquid is called sugar sap.

In autumn, the sugar maple's leaves turn bright red, orange, and yellow before they fall off the tree. During the winter, the sugar maple stops growing. The tree is **dormant**, which means "not active," or "asleep."

sugar maple leaves
in summer

In March, when the temperature gets warmer and the snow melts, the sugar maple wakes up from its sleep and starts growing new leaves.

But all of these new leaves need food to keep growing, so the sugar sap that the tree has been storing from the previous summer begins to flow inside the trunk. Some people collect sugar sap from sugar maples and make maple syrup out of it.

This man is collecting maple syrup from sugar maples.

21

wildflowers

Autumn isn't the only time when the deciduous forest is colorful. In the spring, the forest floor is covered with wildflowers. These wildflowers have a very short life. They must complete their flowering before the summer, when the trees above will be covered with leaves. During the summer, the leaves block sunlight from reaching the forest floor. Then wildflowers cannot make enough food to live.

PLANT PROFILE

Name: yellow ladyslipper orchid

Biome: The woodlands of the eastern United States

Interesting Facts: During the 1800s, the yellow ladyslipper was used as medicine to relieve pain. It is now rare and should not be picked in the wild.

yellow ladyslipper orchids

The **Grasslands**

grasslands

Some parts of the world are flat and covered by tall grass rather than trees. These grasslands are usually wet during part of the year, but dry at other times. During the dry months, they may burn from fire started by lightning. Trees need a long time to grow, so the fires keep trees from moving in and taking over. The ash from the fire gets mixed with the soil. The ash is good for the grass, so it grows even taller.

Fire plays an important role in the grassland biome.

Grasslands are home to many large animals.

CHAPTER 6

In tropical areas, like Africa, grasslands are called **savannas**. In other places, including parts of the midwestern United States, these grassy biomes are called **prairies**. Grasslands are home to some very large animals, such as elephants in Africa or bison in the United States.

An elephant stands in the tall grasses of the African savanna.

24

Animals in the grasslands eat a lot of grass, but this does not destroy the biome. The grass has a special way of growing.

While most plants produce new leaves at the tips of their stems, grasses grow from the bottom. If the top of a grass plant is cut by the teeth of a rhinoceros (or by a lawn mower), it does not die. It simply keeps growing from the bottom.

These bison feed on prairie grass.

PLANT PROFILE

Name: purple coneflower

Biome: The purple coneflower was once common in the prairie grasslands of North America before most of this biome was destroyed for farming.

Interesting Facts: Although rare in the wild, purple cone-flowers are cultivated in gardens for their beautiful flowers. A medicine made from the root of this plant is used to treat the common cold.

purple coneflowers

25

7 The **Desert**

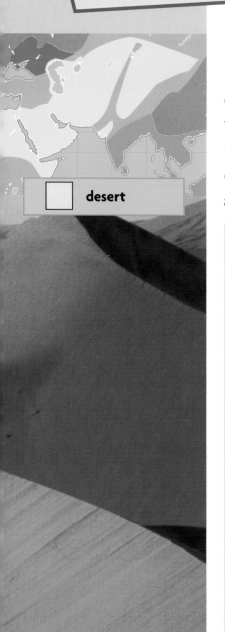

desert

Close your eyes and picture a desert. Do you see a hot, dry, sunny place covered in sand and without plants? You might be surprised to know that many remarkable plants can be found even in the hottest and driest deserts of the world.

Mojave Desert in California

One of these plants is the cactus. Cacti (more than one cactus) are perfectly adapted for life in the desert biome. They have no leaves, but they have thick, green stems that soak up sunlight and store water inside.

It's a FACT!

The average daily temperature at Alice Springs Desert Park in Australia is 97° Fahrenheit (36° Celsius) in summer. At night it drops to 70° F (21° C). During the winter, it can reach 67° F (19° C) during the day, and 9° F (-12° C) at night. For the entire year, only 1.1 inches (2.8 centimeters) of rain falls.

These are cacti in a North American desert.

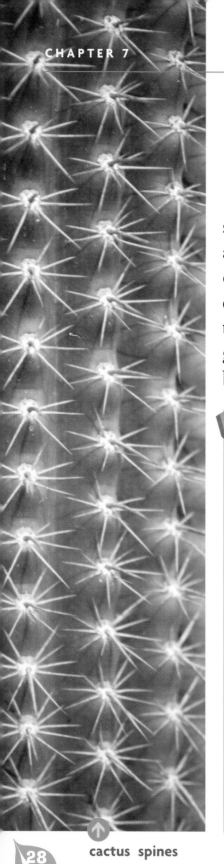

CHAPTER 7

Most cacti are covered with sharp spines. These are for protection against animals that would love to take a bite out of the cacti's juicy stems. Many desert plants also produce a long **taproot** that grows deep into the ground. The taproot finds water deep beneath the surface of the ground.

PLANT PROFILE

Name: saguaro (suh-GWAHR-oh) cactus

Biome: Grows only in the Sonoran Desert of the southwest United States and Mexico

Interesting Facts: This is the largest cactus in the world. It grows 4 to 8 inches per year. The biggest is about 45 feet tall. It can live to be 200 years old. It produces waxy, white flowers with a strong, sweet smell. These flowers open only at night and are visited by bats that feed on the flower's nectar.

saguaro cactus

cactus spines

Deserts are found in many different parts of the world. But plants in the cactus family are found only in deserts of North America and South America.

If you visit a desert in Africa, you will see plants that have no leaves and are covered with spines. They look like cacti, but they are not. The crown-of-thorns is an example. How do we know this plant is not a cactus? Scientists classify plants according to their flowers. Even though both the cactus and the crown-of-thorns have thorns, their flowers are completely different.

beavertail cacti in Escalante River Canyon, Utah

crown-of-thorns plant

8 Plants Around You

When you are outdoors, look at the plants you see growing around you. Think about how they are adapted to their biome.

Then, go to a garden store, and look at the plants for sale. Many of them come from different biomes. Choose one you like, and ask how best to grow it. If you decide to buy it, make sure it has the proper water, sunlight, soil, and air temperature. Make its home as much like its natural biome as you can.

Glossary

adapted	suited to live in a certain place
air plants	plants that grow on tree branches
Arctic	the land closest to the North Pole
biomes	regions of Earth that have their own kind of climate, soil, plants, and animals
buttress roots	special roots that spread out above ground to hold up a tree
canopy	the upper part of a forest of trees
deciduous trees	trees that drop their leaves in autumn
dormant	not active; asleep
drip tip	the tip of a leaf that lets water drip away
equator	the imaginary line that goes around the middle of Earth
evergreen	word used to describe a plant that does not drop its leaves in autumn
lichen	an organism that is part plant and part fungus
prairies	grasslands in a cool *temperate* place
savannas	grasslands in a warm *tropical* place
taproot	long root that grows deep into the ground
temperate	not very cold or very hot
tropical	very hot and humid

Index